The
Bear

Published by Raintree Steck-Vaughn Publishers, an imprint of Steck-Vaughn Company.

Acknowledgments
Project Editor: Helene Resky
Design Manager: Joyce Spicer
Consulting Editor: Kim Merlino
Consultant: Michael Chinery
Illustrated by Robert Morton
Designed by Ian Winton and Steve Prosser
Electronic Cover Production: Alan Klemp
Additional Electronic Production: Bo McKinney and Scott Melcer
Photography credits on page 32

Planned and produced by The Creative Publishing Company

Library of Congress Cataloging-in-Publication Data
    Crewe, Sabrina
    The bear / Sabrina Crewe ; [illustrated by Robert Morton].
       p.   cm. — (Life cycles)
    Includes index.
    Summary: Describes the habitat, food, and life cycle of the black bear.
    ISBN 0-8172-4367-4 (hardcover).   ISBN 0-8172-6230-X (pbk.)
    1. Bears — Juvenile literature.   2. Black bear — Juvenile literature.   3. Bears — Life cycles — Juvenile literature.   4. Black bear — Life cycles — Juvenile literature.   [1. Black bear.   2. Bears.]   I. Morton, Robert.   II. Title.   III. Series: Crewe, Sabrina. Life cycles.
    QL737.C27C745   1997
    599.74'446 — dc20   96-4845
                                       CIP   AC

1 2 3 4 5 6 7 8 9 0 LB 00 99 98 97 96
Printed and bound in the United States of America.

Words explained in the glossary appear in
bold the first time they are used in the text.

LIFE CYCLES

The
Bear

Sabrina Crewe

RSVP

RAINTREE
STECK-VAUGHN
P U B L I S H E R S
The Steck-Vaughn Company

Austin, Texas

The mother bear is in her den.

The mother bear is sleeping. Two cubs have been born in the **den** during the winter. At first, the tiny cubs have no teeth and almost no fur. They cannot see.

The cub is leaving the den.

Spring has come. The cubs are
a few months old. It is time to
go outside.

The mother bear nurses her cubs.

The cubs are feeding on their mother's milk. For the first few months, this is all they eat.

The cub has found some food.

Now the bear cubs are old enough
to try other food. They learn to look
for young plant **shoots** and insects.
Sometimes they find birds' eggs, too.

The cubs are exploring.

Bear cubs spend a lot of
time looking at their world.
Everything they see and
smell is new and interesting.

The cubs play together.

Cubs like to wrestle and chase each other.
When cubs play, they are learning **skills**
that they will use when they are older.
Their games teach them about hunting
and looking after themselves.

The mother bear is angry.

The mother bear watches while her cubs play. She is teaching them how to stay safe. She wants them to know it is dangerous to wander away from her.

The cubs are in the tree.

The mother bear has sensed danger. She sends the cubs up into a tree. She will stay on the ground to protect them.

The cubs are eating berries.

It is fall. The cubs eat as much as they can. They need to **store** fat in their bodies, because they won't have much to eat when winter comes. Besides berries, the cubs eat insects, fish, and other animals.

The mother bear looks for a den.

Bears need **shelter** when it gets cold.
Bears seem bigger in the winter. Their
fur grows thick to keep them warm.

The bears are sleeping.

The mother bear has made a
den under a rock. She has lined
the den with leaves and twigs.

The cubs stay with their mother through
the winter. The bears sleep most of
the time. Sometimes they wake up and
go for walks to find food.

The bear is marking a tree.

It is spring, and the bears have left the den. The young bear is using its sharp claws to scratch marks on tree trunks. This will show other bears that they are in this bear's **territory**.

Bears live alone.

Bears live by themselves after leaving their mothers. They leave when they are two years old and choose their own territory.

The bear is following a trail.

Bears travel long distances to look
for food. They use the same trails
many times. This helps them find their
way back to good feeding places.

The bear has caught a salmon.

Bears stand in the river and watch
for fish. When a fish comes close,
the bear moves quickly. It catches
the fish with a paw or in its mouth.

Bears love honey.

It is summer. The bear has found a bees'
nest inside a tree. It dips into the nest
with its paw to pull out the honey.

The bees protect their nest. They will
try to sting a bear that takes their
honey. But it can be hard for bees to
get through a bear's thick fur and skin!

The bear has found some garbage.

Bears can cause trouble when they look for food. They will **raid** camps and garbage cans. Sometimes, bears even go into houses!

The bear senses humans.

The bear stands up on its back
legs to watch and listen. Usually,
bears won't hurt anyone who
leaves them alone. But they
may attack if people or
animals come too near.
Never try to feed a
bear in the wild.

The bear has found a mate.

Male and female bears spend time together when they want to mate. They don't stay together after they have mated. The cubs will be born while the female is in her winter den.

Bears need wilderness.

Bears need large areas of forest or
mountains in which to live. People
can help bears by protecting **wilderness**.
Then bears will have enough land to
find food and raise their young.

Parts of a Bear

Bears belong to a group of **mammals** called **carnivores**. Like other mammals, carnivores have fur and feed their young with milk. All carnivores are hunters. They have sharp claws and teeth, and their bodies are strong. Most carnivores eat only meat. Some, including bears, eat plants as well.

Thick fur
For protection and warmth
Grows thicker for the winter

Small eyes
Sight is weak.

Nose
Very good sense of smell for finding food and identifying danger

Sharp teeth
Large front teeth for tearing meat
Flat back teeth for chewing plants

Curved claws
Good for digging for food and climbing trees

Other Carnivores

Polar bear

Grizzly bear

Sloth bear

The bears in this book are American black bears. Here are some other bears and different kinds of carnivores.

Mountain lion

Raccoon

Badger

Wolf

29

Where the American Black Bear Lives

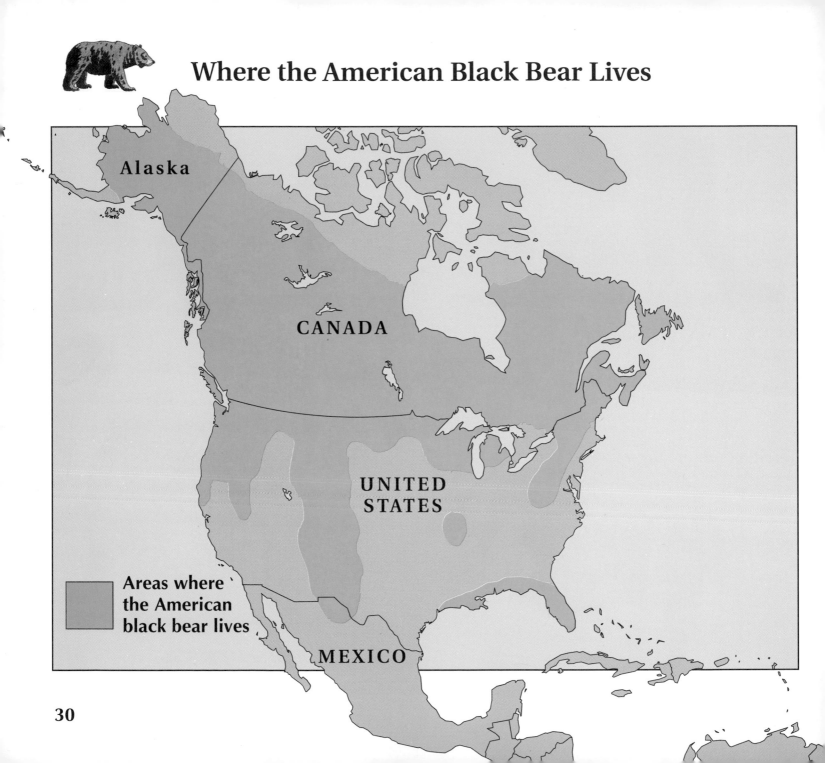

Alaska

CANADA

UNITED
STATES

Areas where
the American
black bear lives

MEXICO

Glossary

Carnivore A type of mammal that has sharp claws and teeth, and that hunts and eats meat

Den The place where a wild animal lives or has its babies

Mammal A kind of animal that usually has fur and feeds its young with milk

Raid To go into a place to take things, such as food

Shelter A place that protects

Shoot The new growth of a plant

Skill The ability to do something well

Store To put something away until it is needed

Territory An area of land that an animal defends as its own

Wilderness A place where people have not lived, built, or farmed

Index

Photography credits

Cover: (top left) Zig Leszczynski/Animals Animals/Oxford Scientific Films; (middle left) Bill Lea/Dembinsky Photo Association/FLPA; (bottom left) Breck P. Kent/Animals Animals/Oxford Scientific Films; (right) Daniel J. Cox/Oxford Scientific Films.

Title page: Mark Newman/FLPA; p. 4: Daniel J. Cox/Oxford Scientific Films; pp. 5 & 6: Zig Leszczynski/Animals Animals/Oxford Scientific Films; p. 7: Ray Richardson/Animals Animals/Oxford Scientific Films; p. 8 (left): Tim Davis/Photo Researchers/Oxford Scientific Films; p. 8 (right): Daniel J. Cox/Oxford Scientific Films; p. 9: Ray Richardson/Animals Animals/Oxford Scientific Films; p. 11: Bill Lea/Dembinsky Photo Association/FLPA; p. 12: Daniel J. Cox/Oxford Scientific Films; p. 13: Frank Schneidermeyer/Oxford Scientific Films; p. 14: John Serrao/Photo Researchers/Oxford Scientific Films; pp. 16 & 17: Daniel J. Cox/Oxford Scientific Films; p. 18: Mark Newman/FLPA; p. 19: Pat and Tom Leeson/Photo Researchers/Oxford Scientific Films; p. 22: Alan Carey/Photo Researchers/Oxford Scientific Films; p. 23: Breck P. Kent/Animals Animals/Oxford Scientific Films; p. 24: Daniel J. Cox/Oxford Scientific Films; p. 25: Tim Davis/Photo Researchers/Oxford Scientific Films.